And Even if We Did, So What?

Poems by

The NÜ Profits of P/o-/e/t/i/c Di$chord

OAC Books
Belle, MO
osageac.org

Copyright © 2021, Jason Baldinger, Damian Rucci, Shawn Pavey, Nathanael William Stolte
First Edition: 1 3 5 7 9 10 8 6 4 2
ISBN: 978-1-952411-66-3
LCCN: 2021942054

Author photos: Alanna Miles, Rosie Lindsay, Naomi Pavey, Maria Lazcano
All rights reserved. No part of this publication may be reproduced or transmitted in any form or by any means, electronic or mechanical, including photocopying, recording or by info retrieval system, without prior written permission from the author.

Acknowledgments:

Jason Baldinger: Some of these poems have previously appeared in *Winedrunk Sidewalk, As It Ought To Be, Rustbelt Review, Vox Populi, Lunch Bucket Brigade* and the *Rye Whiskey Review*

Damian Rucci: Thanks to *As it Ought To Be Magazine, Horror Sleaze Trash, Sledgehammer Lit, Anti-Heroin Chic, Daily Drunk Magazine, Soup Can Magazine, Big Hammer* & *Eunoia Review*

Shawn Pavey: "Letter to My Poet Friends in Quarantine," "On Learning How to Play Chuck Berry's Johnny B. Goode on Guitar," "Dick Dale Cures the 'Rona,"– *The Rye Whiskey Review*
"Mayfly on the Glass Door of My Studio in the Glow of an Outdoor Bulb," "Birds and Poems" – *Polarity Magazine*
"Mo(u)rning Ghazal," "The Day After Armistice Day," "Basic Economy ," "Ghazal of Regret" – *Rusty Truck*
"Hypothesis: Every Night is Friday Night (When Unemployed)," "Emerging New Is Old Hat," "The Costco Poem," "Channeling Ryberg" – *The Gasconade Review,*
"Charles Bukowski Is Dead" – *As It Ought To Be*

Nathanael William Stolte: Some of these poems have been previously published in *Black Coffee Review* & *Thimble Literary Magazine.*

TABLE OF CONTENTS

Jason Baldinger

perfect yinzer / 1
this time sparrows will fly out / 2
overnight windmill / 4
the recession virus blues / 6
time is dead / 8
this poison heaven / 10
hymn to chickaree hill / 12
it's the laser beams again / 13
this isn't rain / 15
another clever species / 17
tube city nightmare / 19

Damian Rucci

Everyone is Wearing Masks and
   It's Not Even Halloween / 23
You Never Realize You're Dancing Alone
   Until the Music Stops / 24
Another Skeleton to Step Over / 25
And Even If I Did, So What? / 27
This Illness / 29
We're Cooking and We're Not Even Chefs / 31
Did We Ever Make It Out of Atlantic Street? / 33

For the Parking Lot Kids / 36
The Weekend Kept Getting Longer / 38
Meeting Crazy Mark at His Wife's Funeral / 39
Something to Write About / 41

Shawn Pavey

On Learning How to Play Chuck Berry's
   Johnny B. Goode on Guitar / 45
Birds and Poems / 47
Ghazal of Regret / 48
Basic Economy / 49
The Costco Poem / 50
Charles Bukowski is Dead / 52
Mayfly on the Glass Door of My Studio
   in the Glow of an Outdoor Bulb / 53
Emerging New is Old Hat / 54
Dick Dale Cures the 'Rona / 55
Worst Superhero Ever: a found poem / 57
Letter to My Poet Friends in Quarantine / 59
The Day After Armistice Day / 60
Libraries Are Their Own Churches / 61
Mo(u)rning Ghazal / 62
Hypothesis: Every Night is Friday Night
   (When Unemployed) / 63
Channeling Ryberg / 64

Nathanael Stolte

Be Kind to the Dishwasher / 67

Chef Days / 68

Lifer / 72

Sink or Swim Nightmare / 74

Tuesdays at Denny's / 75

Rome / 76

Thirteen Ways of Looking at Your
  Student Teacher / 78

It Rained From Columbus to Nashville / 81

Crazy Mark / 83

New, but Borrowed / 84

Lonesome Blood Clot / 86

He used to carry his guitar in a gunny sack
Go sit beneath the tree by the railroad track
Oh, the engineers would see him sitting in the shade
Strumming with the rhythm that the drivers made
The people passing by they would stop and say
Oh my what that little country boy could play

-Chuck Berry, *Johnny B. Goode*

Jason Baldinger

Jason Baldinger is from Pittsburgh and misses roaming the country writing poems. His newest book is *A Threadbare Universe* (Kung Fu Treachery Press). Forthcoming books include *The Afterlife is a Hangover* (Stubborn Mule Press) and *A History of Backroads Misplaced* (Kung Fu Treachery). His work has been published widely across print journals and online. You can hear him read his work on Bandcamp and on lp's by The Gotobeds and Theremonster.

perfect yinzer

they're making out
hot and heavy
swallowing tongues
in astro vans

wind blows
a ticker tape parade
of xerox signs
safety, patience
sorry, love

anarchist scutter
across streets
people gust along
tumble weeds blank-eyed
spinning in the dark

two old men
own their stoop
one in perfect yinzer

itz friday night
an no onez aht
itz a gawdam ghostahn

his buddy returns
everrwher' iz

this time sparrows will fly out

it's been a year since
I woke up in nashville
on the floor of a revolution
that couldn't be seen
on the floor with chipmunks,
the sparrows, the smell of fall
in the dead leaves of an old hickory tree

here we are with all this loss
her hands no longer turn to crows at dawn
her old lover dead again
she has guilt, she has resentment
you can build a life there
but goddamn it isn't a place
any of us could, or should, stay

somewhere out there
the romance of americana
can still be held with the eyes
with this fading season arrived
with all good things wrapped in breath
adieu false heart

the other day the conversation
turned to anxiety, this is what we talk
about when we talk about now

let me open my hands
this time sparrows will fly out
will overwhelm a world of beech trees

our illnesses myriad in this light
goddamn, are as tired as I am
do you find the word tomorrow
heavy as damp stars
does it seem strange to you
when you say tomorrow out loud
like it's already here, like it'll never arrive
say it with me now, it might be alright

overnight windmill

twenty years on the road
still can't sleep in motels
without a television
to distract the ghosts
tonight, I trust edibles
to send me below the surface

reality is a nuisance
in the next room
headboard in rhythm
as a couple engage
her muffled instructions
I rifle through my bag in the dark

between the toilet, the tub
vent fan glows cherry red
blow smoke into the bowl
discreet

I return to sleepless
the bed in the next room
sounds like it climaxed alone

back to drift momentarily
the heat unit in this room climaxes
a noticeable burning

fire alarm screams
leap up stoned
flail with shirt at detector
overnight windmill
clear back to silence

smoke lingers
listen for the next round of ghosts

rabbit heart, slow blood
this last days boogie
the tumult of multiple pandemics

time applies to half the room
I retreat under a blanket of smoke
hope for the privilege
to wake up alone
in a motel south
of south williamsport

my death
thankfully is not here
I've seen it
in headlights, in rearview
it's still miles away

the recession virus blues

it's the same strange feeling
whether you want the job
whether you were ready to quit
whether the next job is waiting
when you hear it again
... *laid off...*

it's that feeling of watery knees
the way the room blurs
air busts out of lungs
desperate not to be trapped
walk in circles, listless
an imposed value snuffed

I don't identify my life
and my work together
I consider myself an artist
working to maintain
the goal of making art
that I don't make money from

I don't identify my life with my job
but in these desperate times
it's clear we are vessels
to a system that expects two things
produce and consume

what happens when both
streams dry up?

a friend texted
the apocalypse is
one long business meeting

she's right, like filing
unemployment in the nineties
first of the morning forms
staring down a bulletin board
of lost manufacturing jobs
scribble assignment numbers
filling applications, waiting
endlessly for an interview
a determination to come

morning birds chorus
out my bedroom window
a slow century of traffic
there's nowhere to be

sorry to say
right now I am not capital
capitalism has no use for me

time is dead

time died quietly
no friends or family
by the bed
no obituary
no news
no sound bite

it had been terminal
what killed it is unsure
autopsy inconclusive
it had been stretched thin
since the industrial revolution
when people were lined up
at the nearest clock
told if they punch it
they'd be given value

seems strange
that time is dead
how lost strangers
are without it
they walk streets
enjoy the sun
confused by life
without structure
every second evaporates
into a beautiful nothing

time is dead
the future is uncertain
because time's past meaning
cannot be retained

time is dead!
time is dead!
freedom for us!

this poison heaven
(for richard houff)

there are a thousand ways
to match this heavy gray sky
a blanket suffocating light

no lift in my step
rather not even wear pants
let alone go outside
stare at sun through gauze
breath with weights on my chest

with sunset desolation comes
I long for passing taillights
something other than wind
tearing at house siding
breaking branches

blooming trees
white flowers whip
across night's palette
a shaking of plague masks

the smell of cigarettes
I wish for the perfume
of a fine dominican cigar

between gusts
a sparrow breaks wind
my eyes spin

across darkness
see a cherry glow

this poison heaven
watches
wonders
if I'm alive

hymn to chickaree hill

that blood red lit
neon is the only
light in the darkness
of chickaree hill

jesus saves
floods the windshield
floods the highway
maybe tonight he does

hang a left
in the turning lane
headlights spin u-turns
gravel pop pop until
the car drifts to park

ascend the steps of golgotha
spread arms in moonlight and red
reach for the knob
the hem of his garment
only to find it locked

jesus may save
this place may offer sanctuary
but only during business hours

it's the laser beams again

it's the laser beams again
chasing an unreliable narrator
wonder about damage of smoking cactus
as world turns to purple pixels
disappear into never
then return to this meat sack
on the back of a colony of bats

yeah, the dinosaur was there
wandering mushroom huts
wearing chuck taylor all stars dopey
I can't stand this dingey kitchen
my brain hemorrhaging light
tendrils of eons beaming
through the night sky
into a flatbed of stars

I dive deep
conscious of every nerve
put out the fire in my jawbone
swim the ocean at the center of earth

I am a fledgling
to whatever reality
conforms to this whim
headlights are laser beams again
north and west
north and unreliable
a black hole in the interstate

now the grid stretches across aisles
gonna need cigarettes
gotta remember money exists
this cashier has no light in their eyes

there's a double coupon special
somewhere in the bardo.

this isn't rain

this isn't rain
doesn't talk like rain
its voice sinister
drowning in clear purpose

out of the farmhouse
a world unfamiliar
saturated skyline sinks
lake swells

the walleye, the trout
can't escape their cages
sermonize all the dreams
of privileged fish bellies

I'm picking berries
like it's the bottom
of the ocean in june

italians wash out of tents
of course laborers couldn't
be offered a dry bed
they swear in dialect
court mud with shovels
antiquated prayers

they watch water
water watches them

atoms still in the flow of waiting
a preordained moment
no one needs permission

rising
the crest is coming
an otherworldly cacophony
of white caps whisper
a sum of panic

it's only mud
it's only mud

another clever species

I dreamed the ocean came for me
it jumped its shore in waves rising
to scrub the virus of humanity

a wall of water came unexpectedly
towered over
swallowed
sucked under
cars and people slam together
dread
foam
panic

I stare up a wall of water
think about lew welch
the red monk, his visions

I'm about to lose everything
I've already lost everything
I never had anything
there is never anything but loss

I stood there
non-combatant in the flow of enemy fire
no future in high ground
waiting my turn at never

but the ocean didn't want me

this is what we to look forward to
as our petty imaginations
ignore the warnings of a planet
we never could see beyond waiting to die
we are hubris embodied
another clever species

tube city nightmare

to get the news
in an old man bar
as a cheese steak drops

eye contact, stomach dips
wave in the bullfight
or run out in the night
chicken without a head
as frost descends

I'd love another beer
we're all gonna die
so drink up, try not to breathe
who cares if the waitress shames you

I pad the tip
sorry for the waste
that has come

in a motel
casting invisibility
and protection spells

I dream of brie and her face shield
myriad instruction
count to fifteen before
dna runs off in tubes

were all gonna die
with the romero crowd
in this tube city nightmare

I've been invisible too long
waiting in nightmares
give a call sometime
service here is spotty
I'll do my best to cut
a signal through the noise

Damian Rucci

Damian Rucci is the author of 5 chapbook of poetry including *Corrupt the Youth* by Between Shadows Press. His work has been featured across the internet and in print. He is a founding member of the Nu Profits of Poetic Dischord, a beer guzzling bard, and probably banned from your local bar.

Everyone is Wearing Masks and It's Not Even Halloween

it's later than that now, the leaves
have fallen across idle and empty streets
smiles are now forbidden fruits
eyes, the last bastion of contact
I never knew how much
I used to read lips

my brother has been reading lips
since 1996, the world a muffled
boombox on the edge of the cosmos
a floating mural of yearning
I know beauty still lingers
on the edge of quiet contemplations

all the coffee shops are closed
all the parties are over
the world is hushed like a first snow
my footsteps echo alone on Myrtle avenue
there is nothing normal about this newness
but there is no resolve but to submit

You Never Realize You're Dancing Alone Until the Music Stops

and you've been living in some kind of mirage
playing dominoes with the devil
you owe the sonofabitch about three fifty
but you both know neither of you are
good at paying debts, the machinery of night
is the only music you need, the demons are on
now dropping from your shoulder to circle
the room taking bets and hollering
you don't even think to leave the table
all your angels must be on vacation or worse
have left your side to stay up all night
with better company, who're you to judge?
You're on, you're here now, the fire in your belly
is out but you have lightning in your veins
sinister breeze on your scalp and a cock that could
cut diamonds, but you're girl is tired of your shit
too, asleep in the next room, your mama
always told you no good man is awake at 3 am,
so what does that make you? Flipping tiles
chain smoking cigarettes and haunting the house
even ghosts have an ambition to scare, you're
a shell and the devil will leave you too as the sunbeams
wake the goodhearted from their sleeps
you'll be walking to that same gas station
to get the same pack of smokes watching the same mothers
send the same kids to school and you will walk back
alone to sleep while the world is awake again

Another Skeleton to Step Over

Diogenes could never tell
the difference between the bones
of the slaves or of the kings
and what makes me any different?

The stories I carry in the shadows
of my bleeding heart aren't novel
the cross I carry on my back is second-hand
I picked it up to see Missouri sunsets and rot

I walk the asphalt via dolorosa looking
to feed my habits, my crown of thorns
is a crown of jackals, I'm never at peace
only when the moon hangs high

and my memories play out in the shadows
vignettes of a past I'm not really sure of
times when the breeze blew gentle
on my back and laughter cured it all

but I'm still walking, the houses I pass
are monuments of joy I will never reach
the people in the windows sit down for dinner
they toast to another evening, I look away

I sing poesy and kick cans towards my undoing
the prodigal son returned and nobody cared
I sent myself to exile and came back a stray
just another skeleton to step over

another skeleton waiting to turn to dust

And Even If I Did, So What?

I guess you have me figured out,
I never shot the sheriff but
I sure as hell broke the toilet
I've prowled empty streets
for baggies of white trash divine
I've breathed the Atlantic and cursed the sky.

I've played robin hood so we could eat
and I'm not sorry, I'd do it again
I've chased country sunsets without
ever thinking to look back towards home
I went searching for myself and got lost.

I've quit every job I've ever had
I've spit in the face of convention
and paid the price of your indignation.
My heads been wet with the midnight dew;
my shoes have worn down from running away
I swing for home runs every chance I get
I know one day I'm going to hit the ball.

I've rolled boulders up and down suburban hills
and searched for honest men at twilight
I've traded my teeth just to get off
can you believe it? My tooth-fairy
is a tweaker with a heart of gold.

I've made best friends in fist fights
and buried the myths I held sacred
in unmarked graves in Indiana
I've been rich in fleeting moments
and so poor I couldn't afford
to pay mind to any of your concerns

I've lost faith in myself and found it
right where I left it under all of my baggage.
I walked into the belly of the beast
and walked out with the mother fucker's
head in my hands

what I guess I'm trying to say is,
I don't regret a single thing.

This Illness

I watch the cars
up and town Broadway
across from Cag's bicycles
I wonder how many drive
idle with heavy hearts?

How many drift aimless
home from work with
grease burned into their arms
with tears scarred into the
corners of their eyes?

You can scrub the dirt from
your skin but you can't clean
this illness from your bones.

I am sick and she is sick
and we were born into this sick world.
The medicine men on the corners
hold our dreams and aspirations,

we've traded Californian vistas
and white fences for landscapes
of death and urban rot.

Tonight I say I am going to kill myself
I've said this every night for months
and with each haunted evening
I tiptoe closer to oblivion
with the faith of a preacher.

We're Cooking and We're Not Even Chefs
for Rich Hyner

enough of this and you cure the longing
enough of this and you can find yourself
building mountains out of piles of dust
building meaning from the endless despair
but with this we are not broken
we are constellations of trauma and loss
we are cogs in a sinister corporate machine
we are doing just fine until the drugs are gone
but even swan songs have gentle melodies
so we hum and laugh and stumble over the words
like it's not the only damned tune we know

we live by the golden rules of the ones before us
what goes on in this room stays in this room
& you're not a junkie if you're wearing your work boots
& that the counter in the closet isn't for eating
but for following lines to their own conclusions
just like we're doing, following each balloon to heaven

in the blood on the floor, our reflections
paint scarlet vignettes of better men
who great each morning clean and innocent
praying to their twelve-step totems
but that life was never meant for men like us
we were born to drink our pain from the work nights
to climb out of the gutter where we were born
to make the whole damn neighborhood proud
to greet each morning with our heads above our hauntings

the real truth is something that can't be spoken
the sins of our fathers are scarred on our souls
we built ourselves from the ruins of other men's dreams
you can clean up your act but your eyes carry the burden
and ours hold the stories that only come out at night
when the party is over and our work boots are off
and the liquor outweighs our reservations
at twilight is when the dogs come out of the men
and we can curse the heavens and tilt our hats
to hell, and the silence that befalls us says it all

Did We Ever Make It Out of Atlantic Street?

I think of you
when I walk down Atlantic Street

I look to the intersection of Church
I see no God but I can still see you
at the end of your driveway
ten years old; angelic and innocent

when I lived in the apartment
on the third floor by the bodega
I would bounce a ball
I would watch the clouds
I would wait for you
to come outside

and we would play
until the street lights came on
talk about the silly things
those odd ten year old things
until your father's screams
would break the quiet

Did we ever really make it
out of Atlantic street?

You a single mother
at twenty four

lost somewhere deep
in the cracks of the system
trying to make magic
out of the crumbs that
fell into your lap

while I'm swimming
in pipe dreams,
working dead end jobs
writing poems in the spaces
between the shifts

we were but the sums
of the leftover parts
of broken dreams
our mothers killing themselves
chaining themselves
to any job that kept
food in the refrigerator

our fathers never intended
to watch us grow up
yours at the kitchen table
smoking pills off aluminum foil
while we played catch
in the backyard

as my father
fashioned nooses
out of polyester flags
of surrender in protective custody
where do the days go now?

I close my eyes as I pass the bodega
in between the bird songs, I can
almost hear our laughter

frozen in time, etched into the sidewalks
forever a picture of innocence
a memory of times now forgotten

For the Parking Lot Kids

Don't listen to what they say;
you know the ones, the beautiful,
the clean faced, the scornful eyed
yuppies whose parent's blood money
bought them a lease on the good life.

Their path was never meant for you,
their bridges are made with gold,
their teeth are porcelain, their homes are warm,
they have never met the world as a stranger.
But you're still out there, in that parking lot,

burying your dreams with pitchers of disbelief—
doing the same shit with the same people
like you weren't meant to cast a shadow,
living a life that you never agreed to
makes you greet death as nothing but a fool.

Even grains of sand are lifted by the wind,
even bad seeds can grow in fertile soil,
even the damned can be forgiven—
but you'll let another day pass, won't you?
Tell yourself you'll start tomorrow?
Tell yourself that you need a plan?
You don't make your appointment with destiny
you just make sure that you show up.

The only thing worse than fear is regret,
sitting on the fence your whole life just leaves you sore
there's a world beyond this damn parking lot
hell is already filled with men who have never tried
there's a fire in your belly, so what's stopping you?

The Weekend Kept Getting Longer

Singing Queen all the way home
from the Casey's General Store
down Bland Avenue to the art house
maybe we're not the champions
but we are the night, we are alive
drunk on Beast Ice and Missouri twilight
dew, we are vagabonds who have run out of gas money
we are scabbed knee philosophers, we are fools
who refuse to to show up to the cubicle
but we're in god's country and the trumpets
of his angels are the blaring horns of the tractor
trailers driving onward down route 89
we all have a cross to bare and tonight it's you
weighing down our shoulders as we carry you
past the post office to the back porch to smoke
and laugh, the devil would find you first
haunt your bones with late night visions
after that night we'd never see you again
what fate befell you would befall us all
the weekend just kept getting longer
moses wasn't the only one who
never made it into Canaan
we flocked to you like a shepherd
we were destined to get lost

Meeting Crazy Mark at His Wife's Funeral

my fourth day in Missouri
crazy mark found me
on South Alvarado &
asked me if I was one of
them arts people

he wanted me to come
to his wife's funeral
and promised beer and pot
I'm never one to turn down
adventure so I found myself
eleven miles outside of town

joined in a prayer with the preacher
who kept getting her name wrong
in front of the crooked heart
he mowed into the backyard
where they lowered her urn
into the crest between its
awkward bulbous curves

when the redneck ritual was over
crazy mark took to his porch
addressing the weeping bodies
as if they were there for a birthday party
"now that she's done and buried
let's smoke some pot"

we smoked joints of skunk weed
laughing until the sun tucked its head
beneath the foothills and the moon
greeted us with its hollow brilliance
until the Missouri night pulled us
out of the driveway, the heart swaying
with the gentle night breeze
crazy mark's laughing almost
concealed his tears

Something to Write About

I don't hang out with the devil
much anymore but he still calls
from time to time; when it's night
or when its morning or when
these stubborn feet don't wanna move
or when the bed calls me to sleep
before it is even ten pm

I don't tell my girl
but he leaves voicemails every so often
asks me can I even remember
the last time I've tasted three am?
Asks me can I remember the last time
I've felt like Adonis? Been the Uberman?
Grooved my footsteps into the wooden floors?
Can I still get it up without a burning nose?
Do the whispers still keep me up at night?
Do I really feel comfortable
in the realm of the living?

Because I've lived a thousand lives before dusk
I've haunted midwestern cow towns
for cigarettes and adventure
I've sold my last ounce of honor
for a bowl of Elysium in dim-lit rooms
I've slain friends in my hearts
over minor quarrels and burned effigies

of my future in gasoline pyres
linoleum melting from the house
like crystal balls dripping through the hands
of the soothsayers

I'd say I didn't know any better
but I'd be lying, I saw the crash
before I ever even signed my name
but I guess I needed to find my way
I guess I needed to see oblivion
for myself, I guess I needed a scar
I could write about

Shawn Pavey

Shawn Pavey is the author of *Talking to Shadows* (Main Street Rag Press, 2008), *Nobody Steals the Towels From a Motel 6* (Spartan Press, 2015), and *Survival Tips for the Pending Apocalypse* (2019, Spartan Press) which was 1st runner up for the 2020 Thorpe Menn Literary Excellence Award. He co-founded *The Main Street Rag Literary Journal* and served as an Associate Editor. His infrequently updated blog is at www.shawnpavey.com. His books can be purchased from him signed and/or personalized at https://shawn-pavey-poet.square.site/ or wherever one prefers to buy books online).

On Learning How to Play Chuck Berry's *Johnny B. Goode* on Guitar

The first thing to remember
when approaching this material
is that the "e" is silent.

The next most important thing to remember
is that the song is recorded in the key of B flat
because Chuck got tired of his piano player
bitching about how guitar players

always wanted to play
in E or G or D or A
because it's easier to figure
out on the fretboard

but it's hell on piano
trying to remember
whether to play the black keys
or the white ones.

The third most important thing to remember
when playing all those slippery little slides
and bends and hammer-ons and double-stops
is that this is the way he played it that day.

Fourth, but equally as important as anything,
one must remember to rest the index finger

on the B and E strings on the sixth fret
while the thumb rests above the bass E.

And this, this most important thing to remember
when attempting to play Johnny B. Goode,
is that to get it – to really get it –

one should learn every lick
that T-Bone Walker ever played
and then come back
and start over.

Birds and Poems

I could try confetti
and be Giacometti
writing on matchbooks
the entirety of my collected works.

Maybe colored origami
but after it is folded
into sand cranes or penguins
or great blue herons.

Possibly that is what will be:
scribbling poems about birds
that soar and sing, wallow in mud puddles,
drink water from upturned flower blossoms

Birds and poems,
the very same thing
when not wadded up or tossed away,
still-born verses in an overflowing trash bin.

Will they take flight?
Hint at what they are?

A feather tucked behind an ear.
A wing out of the corner of an eye.

Ghazal of Regret

Memories of childhood seem to come in various hues
        of green: Lawn in late
spring, undersides of leaves in shade of that old maple
        near an opened gate.

Which face do we wear now to the world, under
        masks, under pandemic,
under virus, under orders, under undermined orders,
        under fear, under greatness?

Modern times, such modern times these are. All of us
        instantly connected
by phones in our pockets, by watches, by tablets so
        devoutly followed and liked, never sated.

Uneasy to predict, tomorrow. Disease of information
        lacking wisdom and context.
We lock windows. Lock cars. Lock doors and cell
        phones and minds and gates.

To be new again. To be open, again. To be fair and
        just and kind and receptive.
To be children. To be smiling. To be singing. To be
        play and playing. Free. Too late.

Basic Economy

Aisle seat offers nothing
but the illusion
of leg room.

Middle seat, well,
as Sartre tells us,
Hell is other people

to the left and to the right
and me in the middle all
broad shoulders and big ass.

Give me the window.
Let me look at the earth
as we leave it,

climbing and rattling and shaking.
Bouncing over cities and valleys,
let me see we are moving.

Let me see progress
as we ascend through clouds
and emerge to jet above them,

travelling a straight line
from waypoint to waypoint.
Let me see the sun or stars above:

sun I can't afford,
stars I don't deserve.

The Costco Poem

When the register doesn't register
shrink-wrapped frozen scallops
it holds up the line and my wife
is so very much done with Costco.

Sunday mornings, the store doesn't open
until 10. Naomi arrives at 9:30.
She does the shopping, I do the laundry,
so I am home, having slept late,

working my way to the bottom
of a strong pot of coffee, playing
my blue Les Paul while sun shines
through windows open to the breeze

of a temperate March morning.
I hear Naomi's car pull in the drive.
So, setting my guitar in its stand,
I rise to open the door to help unload.

Naomi meets me at the door with the face,
the one that states that I'd better help
and I'd better be quick about it and that a long
hug and a possible cry are in my immediate future.

You see, we do not like crowds. Or people.
Especially, we do not like crowds of people.
And Costco is not supposed to be crowded
on Sundays, it should be near empty. Church.

This is the way we planned it. This is the way
we planned it all along but the churches are closed.
Costco is the new church, toilet paper, the new wafer,
and 2% milk is the new blood of Christ.

Charles Bukowski Is Dead

Follow along. Stay with me.
Charles Bukowski is dead.
We should keep him there, dead,
where his bones lie draped
in a moldering suit.
The drinking and the poems about drinking
are not new. Not to me. Not to you.

The rawness there, the open wound,
the lovers and the unloved and the violent
let them stay in the ground.
Let them stay in the ground
with the moldering suit (we talked
about this). Find a new place to walk
that isn't Los Angeles. Find a new bar
that isn't Los Angeles. Find a new city
that isn't Los Angeles. It's time.
You know it's time.

Mayfly on the Glass Door of My Studio in the Glow of an Outdoor Bulb

Tying flies with my father
in the evenings in the garage,
my vice holding a size 16 hook,
wrapping it in thread and feathers
to look like food for trout.

I could never tie the mayfly right.
Made woolly worms, a simpler fly,
as well as anyone, used them to pull browns
from Rocky Mountain streams.

But the mayfly required a level of intricacy
my young fingers could not achieve.
Pop told me to keep trying.
So I did and I did and I did
and not a single one of them
landed in a river.

Emerging New is Old Hat

We bring ourselves out of bedsheets
each and every expected bright morning,
wash off what we bring from the day before.
What will today offer? Summertime heat?
Kansas winter's ever reaching cold sting?
A frightened rabbit greets us in spring for
a moment just long enough to disappear.

And work piles up, it just never ceases
its ubiquitous and insidious
dread and breath-removing atmosphere
of wanting and failure, triumphs, pieces
of selves we wish to be lie piteous
on cheap and drab industrial carpet floors.
Days drag on and on, a clock ticks, the heart beats.

Dick Dale Cures the 'Rona

for Jason Vivone

Let's just say you had a meltdown in the grocery store
because your hands are so dry from washing and
        sanitizing
that you can't open the plastic produce bags
and your glasses are fogging up from your own
        breath

    escaping through the top of your quickly fashioned
    quarantine mask constructed from cut out swaths
    of an old trade-show t-shirt and elastic hair ties
    and there's no toilet paper on the shelves

    and they're out of the brand of toothpaste
    that has kept you cavity-free since college
    which, now, was more than thirty goddamned
    years ago. Let's say you had that meltdown.

Let's say it's late afternoon on a Thursday
and even though you should be working from home
this trip to the store is the closest thing you've had
to a vacation all year and there's no real work anyway

    and after parking the car, sanitizing the groceries,
    putting the groceries away, and realizing that your
    very public and, now, embarrassing meltdown
    is going to eat at you for weeks, for months
    (let's be real, years),

you turn on the radio and your guitar teacher
who is also a part-time DJ on a local
listener-supported station
starts playing *Miserlou* and *Pipeline* by Dick Dale
and the magic of Fender spring reverb tanks
and single-coil pickups

cures the corona virus blues.

Worst Superhero Ever: a found poem

Florida Man fatally shoots son-in-law
    who was trying to surprise him for his birthday
Florida Man parks smart car in kitchen
    so it won't blow away
Florida Man takes golf cart on wild ride
    through Walmart
Florida Man arrested for threatening
    to shoot up Walmart after El Paso Massacre
Florida Man caught exposing himself
    in Walmart pillow aisle
Florida Man arrested, caught on video
    using samurai sword to fight over wheelbarrow
Florida Man who didn't flush toilet
    threatened griping friend with a machete
Florida Man threatens to kill man with kindness,
    uses machete named "Kindness"
Florida Man doesn't get straw,
    attacks McDonald's employee
Florida Man intentionally drove Ferrari 360 into
    ocean at top speed, says "Jesus told him to"
Florida Man killed ex-girlfriend
    while trying to "get rid of the devil"
Florida Man shooting at target in backyard
    hits neighbor sitting at dining room table
Florida Man denies syringes found in rectum
    are his
Florida Man accused of burning son
    to teach him a lesson about fire

Florida Man allegedly fooled family into believing
    murdered wife was still alive
Florida Man beat, pepper-sprayed Mom
    because "She was a narcissist"
Florida Man finds a WWII grenade, places it in his
    truck, drives to Taco Bell
Florida Man learns hard way
    he stole laxatives, not opioids
Florida Man spent weeks in jail for heroin
    that was actually detergent
Florida Man accused of robbing Chinese restaurant
    at finger point
Florida Man thought he'd do donuts
    on the airport runway
Florida Man dances
    through DUI sobriety test
Florida Man caught on camera
    licking doorbell

Letter to My Poet Friends in Quarantine

Can we write enough poems about Django Reinhardt
It's a question I keep asking myself
Knowing if you were here
Brothers and Sisters you would have treatise
At the ready and in triplicate
So when I hear those thin scratchy recordings
When the violin player takes the solo in
The World is Waiting for a Sunset
And Django way in the back is strumming faster
Than a hummingbird wing
And man he can just make that thing swing
And then in *I Saw Stars* how he's just chopping
Chopping those strings in that mystic rhythm
And man can't he just take you with him
Then when he steps out front
In *Nuages* each note drips out so sweet
That maybe we think this sadness will be forever
But let him slip into a little boogie groove
Like in *Artillerie Lourde* oh let him speak it true
How sometimes the ammo's heavy baby
Sometimes you just have to lay it on down

The Day After Armistice Day

9° Fahrenheit in Kansas City
and the ground is covered in a half inch
of ice and snow.

We haven't had time even
to get the leaves up this year.
Christ, the trees are still turning.

Thanksgiving is more than half a month away
and air in Europe blows quietly for now
as that great first world war ended 101 years ago.

We're still cleaning up the mess.
Still raking the leaves blown about the world
for more than a century, the winds

still howling through barrels of guns.

Libraries Are Their Own Churches

We do not gather in churches, as one might expect
of angels, we do not gather in a glow
of stained glass with its light smelling of incense
where under dust and time sit endless echoes
of prayers both silent and spoken, and hymns
from choir voices, hymns sung by awkward
singers and tone-deaf singers and surprising,
unassuming singers. No.

No, we gather in libraries and listen
to whispers of words in all of these minds
transmuted from ink on pages to words of stories,
words of philosophies, words of mathematics and
words of science and, oh, such poetry, such language
and such music as all these pages and minds can hold
and we gather here and listen to all these minds
become a symphony of thought and discovery
and questions and, ah, connections
and, oh, the great roar
of wanting to know to know to know!
What human
where human
when human
who human
why?

Mo(u)rning Ghazal

Heavy rains for the better part of twenty four hours.
The river rises, water overflowing its borders.

Thunder fills everyone standing with dread, but lightning
cracks the air, opens us to all the sky's murderous powers.

Beside a propane tank behind my studio, at the edge
of an overgrown gravel drive, sway black-eyed Susans
              and lacy wildflowers.

Strong black coffee punctuates overcast mornings.
Cigarettes are good, too, but I don't smoke those anymore.

Last week, chatted with an old and dear friend who's
              writing a book
on "The History of Reading" that I want to devour.

He told me it's cancer. He told me the executor of his will
will send me his lifetime's book collection of analysis and verse.

I do not want my friend to die and neither do I want to end.
I am exhausted from saying goodbye, yet here we are.

Hypothesis: Every Night is Friday Night (When Unemployed)
with apologies to Rhett Miller and the Old 97s

Easiest thing to do when unemployed
for months is to lose track of days
of the week so why not make
every day Friday in your mind
the only problem being the virus
that's killing people on your social media
friends list making you afraid

to leave your house.

Channeling Ryberg

It might be after 3 a.m.
and sleep is a mystery
you've never cracked
and you think of a sandwich
even though your
belt is a little more snug
these days and these days
you want to "avenge the death
of your master" but you can't remember
his or her or their name
not that it ever mattered anyway
so you listen to Son House
with the volume set low
as to not disturb the rest
of your wife who is safely employed
and keeping you from a homeless shelter
and you thank her quietly
and often for the save
and Son sings to you
Oh, the blues is a lowdown old aching chill
If you ain't had 'em boys, I- I hope you never will
but you have had and you do have
that coldness in your bones
that grind and creak and crack of bones
with each rising out of chairs.

Nathanael Stolte

Nathanael William Stolte hails from Buffalo, NY where he spent the pandemic taking shelter in his mother's basement convalescing from a summer heart attack. He did not spend that time wisely. His poems have appeared in various digital and print journals and magazines. He is the author of several chapbooks and *Shoot the Alligators Closest to the Boat* (Stubborn Mule, 2019) & *Beggar's Songbook* (Spartan Press, 2020). Stolte is a sober alcoholic, flower-punk, madcap poet. He replies to emails at nathanaelstolte@yahoo.com

Be Kind to the Dishwasher

Just about anyone
can wash dishes
with some degree
of proficiency

But don't think
for a second
that makes the job
inconsequential

You work a Fish Fry Friday night
or Easter Sunday Morning
with no one in the dish pit
& you'll know

Dish dog is the most important
job in the house

Chef Days

The Sabres are playing at the arena down the street tonight
I got here at 5:30 this morning to unload the truck with
    Tennessee Paul
I won't leave until they drop the puck on the ice tonight

I learned not to interrupt Tennessee when he's talking or
he'll get red in the face
point a finger at your chest & yell
shut your fucking cocksucker & listen
through his teeth

He's a good guy though
fair &
he gets it
how hard it is to work the line
how this job slices you thin
grinds you down & how important it is
to get a smoke break

We'll be working Char tonight
Tennessee & I
we work well together because
I know my place &
I know how to keep my mouth shut & listen

I only work the line on event nights
these days or in a pinch

I do prep work in the kitchen upstairs
following recipes by myself
making
soups
salad dressings
salsa &
barbecue sauce
all from scratch
I even save the vegetable scraps
fat I carve off of freshly roasted beef
& cleave from raw chicken
to make stock

we sold fifteen gallons of my
Chicken Ranchero soup yesterday

I like it up here by myself
with the oldies station on the
cellophane wrapped AM/FM radio
chopping & dicing with Arthur Conley
simmering & stirring with Sam & Dave
weighing & portioning with Don McLean
tighening up with Archie Bell & The Drells
not too tight y'all

It's hot up here
but I've got a box of pink wine I can nip at &
I can smoke on the second floor patio
anytime I want before they open up the bar at 3

On event nights I gotta be down in the main kitchen
before we line it up in the parking lot out back
by the dumpsters

Divide the three lines between the ten cooks
Paul goes over tonight's specials
while we stand in a circle & smoke

Calm before the insanity

Nicky Bones slips me an Adderall on the sly
to swim in the pink wine belly

artificial second wind

there are six bartenders & more than thirty servers
on the schedule tonight
were outnumbered nearly four to one

They're all busy
impatient &
flooding us with orders
I feel like those three-hundred
Spartans holding back the Persian tide

It's all an amphetamine blur
Grill Pantry is in the weeds &
Pizza Fry keeps burning fired bread

Hues Corporation comes on the greasy radio &
I start singing softly
when Tennessee slams the long handled charbroiler
spatula down hard on the edge of the steam table

it rings like a bell
clearing the fog
as he belts out
Our love is like a ship on the ocean
we've been sailing with a cargo of love & devotion
at the top of his lungs

Without missing a beat we all stop & respond with
So I'd like to know where you got the notion

to rock the boat
don't rock the boat baby

& just like that we all laugh & the spell is broken
morale is high & we have what we need to finish out
   the night

Eventually they drop the puck on the ice down the street
& I take off my chef coat
hang it up in my locker &
go upstairs to enjoy a pint of dark
while I wait for the next bus home

Lifer

The guy calling the rail through
the dinner rush tonight
is abusive and unkind
his grey ponytail is unwashed
the smell of his rotten teeth is louder than the
fryer oil that should have been changed last week

He's old
one of them career cooks
been here 30 years & it shows on his face
none of the servers like him much
even the new girl has seen him at his worst &
his best is long gone

I keep my mouth shut &
work the fryer
drop the food he calls out
press the button & wait for
The timer to play my song

I speak only to call out food I put up in the window
Or to tell time left on orders he needs

Let him worry about the rest
I'm too tired to argue with him today

At least he never holds a grudge

30 years on the line will make you tough
he's been rough on the 18 year-old dishwasher working
nights while he goes to college
screaming for dinner plates and vegetable dishes
but he calls them monkey dishes even though that's
against company policy

That kid will get out of this place someday &
so will I

Maybe he's frustrated with the youth
not the boy but youth itself
his is gone
spent sweating in a crummy kitchen for a shred more
than minimum wage

Sink or Swim Nightmare

It's corn starch hot
in the kitchen this summer
there's no AC & the hood fans
have a scab of grease
blocking their suction

The printer won't stop
spitting out tickets &
the new guy keeps fucking up

Why don't they train him during the week?

instead of this Friday night sink or swim nightmare

The servers are rattled
it's rough out there
the lady at table 3-5
has sent her well done steak back twice

make it shoe leather and send it out again

If we can clear the rail
I can burn a Newport by the dumpster
fast as in the bathroom in High School
before I stock the line for round three

Just another Friday night

Tuesdays at Denny's

On September 11th, 2001
they let us bring the small TV/VCR combo
they use for training videos
up on the cooks line so we
could watch the news
while we made
Grand Slams
Moons Over my Hammy &
Ultimate Omelets

Both the other guys working the line with me
swore they would sign up
if we went to war
do their part to defend freedom
get some revenge
really make them pay for what they've done
whoever they are

Time went by &
we worked the line
making
All American Slams
doing our part for Capitalism

Last I heard Pete was in prison for raping his
step-daughter & Kevin was still working the line

That's not my idea of freedom

Rome

Luigi, from San Pellegrino, Italy
peels and pops the top on an
aranciata San Pellegrino as
we sit in the shade of the
back patio of the Tropics
Hostel in Miami Beach
Florida

Luigi, in his black ball-cap
v-neck, black athletic pants
with a single white stripe
that leads to his white
leather shoes, tells us about
his hometown through
exhaled cigarette smoke

Luigi gets that far away
countenance as he looks up
at the Atlantic sky and into the past
he speaks of mountains and family
snow and culture

Luigi returns to the present moment
looks me square in the eyes while he
extends an open hand
palm turned towards the heavens
fingers slightly apart

and raises his hand gently to whisper
Rome
as if he were sharing with me
some ancient bit of magic
some secret
I believe in this moment
that he is

Luigi leans back and sips his
San Pellegrino
takes a deep pull from his Camel cigarette
exhales through his teeth with a hiss

Rome
louder this time
almost a proclamation
a mantra

Luigi tells us about the cyclical nature of empire
of how Rome ruled through culture and force
just like the American Hollywood dominates

Rome
Luigi says
did some good too you know
roads art poetry
if it was still here today I bet it'd be
one big fucking strip mall
just like America

Thirteen Ways of Looking at Your Student Teacher

after Wallace Stevens

I
Neil deGrasse Tyson told me
I was born of matter formed in a distant and ancient star
So were you
Really makes me wonder that life is an absurdly precious gift

II
I found him
Still warm but not breathing
The room filled with his last labored breaths
I breathed deeply through my nose
The air was cold enough to sting
I have been holding my breath ever sense

III
The Baby Boomers are said to be losing their hearing in record numbers
Too much Rock n Roll
I wonder what my generation
The Millennials will suffer
I fear it will be our empathy
Too much screen time

IV
Be grateful I don't teach math
Numbers are an alphabet I will never grasp

V
Daddy used to drink corn whiskey and write sermons
Thick with metaphor
Then he stopped writing
I don't know what he does now

VI
Emoji's are modern hieroglyphs
And no less important
I can't decipher either
Sorry not sorry

VII
The eighteen-wheeler is on its side; the car is on fire
The gunmetal sky delivers tenacious rain
I have nothing to complain about in my
Own troublesome blessings

VIII
The Gasconade River
In the Northern Ozark Mountains
Washed me clean of troubles
But did nothing for my worry

IX
Three blackbirds are picking
At a fresh doe's exposed ribs
They flit to the guardrail

As I drive past
I watch them return to their duty
In the backwards reflection of my rearview
This is an unfavorable omen

X
Pumpkin spice anything is the only problematic aspect of autumn

XI
I opened my eyes for the first time
Under the fixed gaze of the constellation Leo
Before they tore down the Berlin Wall
Before Los Angeles was set ablaze
The internet is a sort of wall
That's a metaphor—
For what keeps us divided

XII
Music is the most pure way to transmit emotion
Poetry and music may not be siblings
But they have the same grandmother

XIII
On January 26, 2011
My circumstances forever changed
In a spreading pool of my own blood
It was the single best thing that has ever happened to me

It Rained From Columbus to Nashville

My last taste of you was Atlantic
ancient recycled salt
that parched lips well before
I lost my gas cap in Georgia

It rained from the Everglades to Tallahassee

with new memories of Alabama
red waddle and pale chicken eggs
stern chicken eyes
Sunday Alabama chicken supper

It rained from Montgomery to Memphis

The house has no mirrors
but the ghosts smell of
chaw and Old Grand-Dad
the knives are dull
the pots are dented
hard water stained

I won't offer the courtesy
of conjuring your name
no more room here for spirits
just sober reflection
kitchen table
black coffee mornings
I washed you off
every dish

every mason jar
every spoon
every hair

It rained until Valentine's Day

Crazy Mark

will do any kind of labor
you got
for twenty dollars an hour

even help bury the bodies

He'll never tell a soul

even if he did
no one would
likely believe him
anyway

he's no liar

he smiles just right
shimmer in those devil blue eyes

so you just never can tell

New, but Borrowed

Though I'm in a new, but borrowed, bed
in a strange land
you've never been to
I still sleep on only half
the old habitual repetition

I know you're not coming

and I'm certainly not
saving it for you
or anyone

not saving it at all
not holding intimate space
for anyone in this dating economy

I leave books of poems
and novels there
that I read before dreaming

all the companionship I require

I don't fix the covers in the morning
never cared much for that

I dream I'm covered in ticks
and they're hungry

growing fat
and round
and gray
and smooth as old river stones
it doesn't itch
but I can't scream
because my teeth are old river stones
round
gray and
smooth
as fattened ticks
and my mouth is full of butterflies
and secrets
too subtle to recall
when the sun rises
like bubblegum over
the far pasture
out the spotted plate glass
picture window

creeping at first
then all at once

I'm not covered in parasites
and my teeth are just fillings

Lonesome Blood Clot

If I was a gambling man
I would have put good money
on the fact that my heart
was nothing more than a potato clock

But on the Fourth of July
when those specialists & that doctor
were suddenly summoned
from whatever family celebration
(following suggested social distancing guidelines, I'm sure)
to thread a camera through my right wrist
& into my heart
like a Roto-Rooter
to find that lonesome blood clot
rattling around like the last Tic-Tac

I watched live on the large monitor
directly above me on my left
the images of my insides
all the way to the heart
when I had to look away in disgust

Maybe it was beautiful

But I just kept wondering
how many beers did this guy have at the BBQ
he probably left to come here?

This project was made possible, in part, by generous support from the Osage Arts Community.

Osage Arts Community provides temporary time, space and support for the creation of new artistic works in a retreat format, serving creative people of all kinds — visual artists, composers, poets, fiction and nonfiction writers. Located on a 152-acre farm in an isolated rural mountainside setting in Central Missouri and bordered by ¾ of a mile of the Gasconade River, OAC provides residencies to those working alone, as well as welcoming collaborative teams, offering living space and workspace in a country environment to emerging and mid-career artists. For more information, visit us at www.osageac.org

www.ingramcontent.com/pod-product-compliance
Lightning Source LLC
Chambersburg PA
CBHW022013120526
44592CB00034B/798